598.41

D1101201

C56 1000 0096 478

HOW DOES IT GROW?

DUCK

Jinny Johnson
Illustrations by Michael Woods

FRANKLIN WATTS
LONDON•SYDNEY

An Appleseed Editions book

First published in 2009 by Franklin Watts
338 Euston Road, London NW1 3BH

Franklin Watts Australia
Hachette Children's Books
Level 17/207 Kent St, Sydney, NSW 2000

© 2009 Appleseed Editions

Created by Appleseed Editions Ltd,
Well House, Friars Hill, Guestling,
East Sussex TN35 4ET

Designed by Helen James
Edited by Mary-Jane Wilkins
Picture research by Su Alexander

All rights reserved. No part of this publication may be reproduced,
stored in a retrieval system or transmitted in any form or by any means,
electronic, mechanical, photocopying, recording or otherwise, without
prior permission of the publisher.

ISBN 978 07496 8786 1

Dewey Classification: 598.4'1

A CIP catalogue for this book is available from the British Library.

Photograph acknowledgements
page 7 E R Degginger/Photolibrary Group; 17 Peter Bisset/Photolibrary Group;
23 Elliott Neep/Photolibrary Group; 29 Ronald Wittek/Photolibrary Group
Front cover Ronald Wittek/Photolibrary Group

Printed in China

Franklin Watts is a division of Hachette Children's Books,
an Hachette UK company.
www.hachette.co.uk

WREXHAM C.B.C. LIBRARY
LLYFRGELL B. WRECSAM

C56 1000 0096 478

MEAC

J 598.41   £

WR

Contents

What's inside

These **creamy-coloured eggs**
have been laid by a **mallard duck**.
Inside each egg a **tiny baby duckling**
is beginning to grow.

There are ten eggs in this nest.
The nest is just a little **hollow**
in the ground. The mother duck has
lined the hollow with **leaves, grass**
and **soft feathers** from her body.

The eggs need to be kept **warm**
and **safe** until they hatch.

MALLARD DUCKS LAY
BETWEEN 8 AND 13 EGGS.

Who looks after the eggs?

Keeping warm

The **mother duck** looks after the eggs. She **sits on the nest** and keeps the eggs **warm** with her body.

She leaves the nest just twice a day. Once in the morning and once in the afternoon **she goes to find food**. Before she leaves she covers the eggs so they don't get too cold.

The mother **turns the eggs** regularly, using her **beak** and her **feet**. She makes sure that every part of the **egg stays warm**.

How long before the eggs hatch?

Ready to hatch

About **four weeks** after the eggs have been laid, they are **ready to hatch**.

A day or two before the eggs hatch, the **ducklings** start to **chirp and squeak** inside the eggs. The mother calls back **quietly**. She stays close and doesn't leave her eggs for a moment now.

Soon a **little crack** appears in an egg. The first duckling is about **to hatch**.

CAN YOU SEE
THE LITTLE CRACK
IN THE EGG?

How does a duckling get out of the egg?

Breaking out

The duckling has to **break free of its shell** on its own. It's not easy. The duckling has a hard tip on its beak, called an **egg tooth**, which it uses to peck its way out.

Once one **egg starts to hatch** the others soon follow. As each duckling **struggles out**, it snuggles under its mum's warm body.

Hatching out is **hard work** and the ducklings need to rest.

ALL THE EGGS USUALLY HATCH ON THE SAME DAY.

What happens next?

First day

The **newly hatched** duckling soon starts to move around the nest. He's steadier on his legs now, but still **stays close to mum**.

The duckling is covered with soft yellow and brown **fluffy down**. This is **damp and sticky** at first and takes about half a day to dry.

Some of the **special oil** on the mother duck's feathers rubs off on her ducklings. This oil makes their downy coats **waterproof**.

When will the ducklings go for their first walk?

Leaving the nest

The day after they hatch,
the ducklings leave the nest
for the first time.

Mum leads her **line** of fluffy
ducklings **to the water**.
She calls to them all the time
and makes sure they **stay in line**.

When they reach the water,
it's time for their **first swim**.

THE DUCKLINGS
MUST BE CAREFUL
NOT TO GET LEFT
BEHIND.

Who feeds the ducklings?

Learning to swim

The **ducklings** can find their
own food from their **first day**.

They take a little while to get used
to swimming. But soon they are
bobbing about on the water,
paddling with their **webbed feet**.

They snap up tiny insects and water
plants with their **broad flat beaks**.

For the first week or so the mother
snuggles up with her ducklings
at night. She keeps them warm
with **her body**.

Do the ducklings still need their mum?

Staying safe

The ducklings **need mum** to keep them safe. She makes sure they all **stay close together** and **quacks loudly** to call them back if any wander too far away.

They can't fly yet so it is hard for them to **escape from danger**, especially when they feed on land. They scuttle about, eating **seeds, worms and snails**. They may leap up to grab insects from the air or from plants.

When they are a few weeks old, the ducklings start to lose their fluffy down and **grow proper feathers**.

When will the ducklings be able to fly?

Learning to fly

By the time they are **eight or nine weeks old** the ducklings have **speckled brown feathers** like their mum's. Their wings have grown bigger and they are **ready to fly**.

A duckling **flaps its wings** as it has seen its mother flap hers and takes off into the air. What a **wonderful** feeling!

Now they can fly the ducklings can look after themselves.

DUCKLINGS USUALLY LEAVE THEIR MOTHER ONCE THEY CAN FLY.

What do the ducks do all day?

A duck's day

The ducks spend their days **feeding, bathing, sleeping** and **cleaning** their feathers.

They are **strong fliers** and can fly up from the water as well as from land. They are **good swimmers** and can **tip upside down** when they look for food.

When they are full grown the **male ducks** look very different from their **sisters**. They have shiny **green feathers** on their heads and reddish-brown chests.

A MALE DUCK IS
CALLED A DRAKE.

When will the duck start its own family?

Finding a mate

Now it is **winter** and the young duck is about nine months old. Soon it will be time for him to **start his own family**.

First he must **show off** to females and attract a mate. Females like males that have bright **yellow beaks** and glossy feathers.

Once the male duck has found a female, they **swim** and **feed** together. A mallard duck feeds by **dipping its head down** and sticking its bottom in the air. In **spring** the pair will mate.

Who makes the nest?

A new family

The female mallard duck prepares **her nest**. She lays her first egg and **covers it up** with grass and feathers. Every day she lays another egg until she has a **clutch**.

Laying eggs is tiring. Her mate stays close by to help **protect her** while she lays eggs, but then **he leaves**.

The female **settles down** to look after her eggs until her **new family** is ready to hatch.

MUM LAYS THE WHOLE CLUTCH BEFORE SHE STARTS TO SIT ON HER EGGS.

More about ducks

What is a mallard duck?
A mallard is a bird which spends at least some of its time in water. It is related to other water-living birds, such as geese and swans. There are lots of other kinds of duck, but the mallard is the most common. There are probably more mallards in the world than any other duck.

Where do mallards live?
Mallards originally lived in North America, Europe and Asia, but now they have spread to many other parts of the world. They are very adaptable and are happy to live in parks in the middle of busy towns and cities.

How big is a mallard?
A full-grown mallard duck is about 50 to 65 cm long and weighs up to 1.3 kg. When its wings are fully spread, they measure up to 95 cm from tip to tip.

A MALE AND
FEMALE MALLARD.
THE MALE HAS A
SHINY GREEN HEAD.

Words to remember

beak

The hard outer part of a bird's mouth.

clutch

A group of eggs laid by a bird.

down

A bird's first soft feathers.

drake

A male mallard.

egg tooth

A little spike on a baby bird's beak, which it uses
to break out of its egg. The egg tooth falls off
a few days after hatching.

hatch

To break out of an egg.

mallard

A type of duck.

mate
Male and female animals pair up, or mate, to produce young. An animal's partner is called its mate.

nest
A place where a bird lays its eggs.

quack
The sound made by a female mallard duck. Males make a slightly different sound.

webbed feet
Feet with flaps of skin between the toes. These make the feet into paddles that help the duck move in water.

Websites

Royal Society for the Protection of Birds
www.rspb.org.uk/wildlife/birdguide/name/m/mallard/

Information and pictures
www.arkive.org/mallard/anas-platyrhynchos/info.html

BBC factfile
www.bbc.co.uk/nature/wildfacts/factfiles/3028.shtml

Index